T0078001

DISCOVERING YOUR UNIQUENESS

"A Young Person's Guide to Discovering Who You Were Created to Be"

SHEILA WHITE

Order this book online at www.trafford.com
or email orders@trafford.com

Most Trafford titles are also available at major online book retailers.

Scripture taken from The Holy Bible, King James Version. Public Domain

Sheila White Skyward Books. A division of Road 2 Eternity Corporation.
Skyward Books 1000 Essington Road, Joliet, Illinois 60435. By email at
info@Skywardbook.com. Visit our website at https://www.SkywardBooks.com.

Manuscript Development Coach: Michael Bart Mathews.
Contact Skyward Books by email at info@Skywardbooks.com to inquire about
how we can help you get your book out of your head so it can be read!

Print information available on the last page.

ISBN: 978-1-6987-0512-5 (sc)
ISBN: 978-1-6987-0514-9 (hc)
ISBN: 978-1-6987-0513-2 (e)

Library of Congress Control Number: 2020925447

Trafford rev. 12/30/2020

Trafford PUBLISHING® www.trafford.com
North America & international
toll-free: 844-688-6899 (USA & Canada)
fax: 812 355 4082

CONTENTS

DEDICATION

I dedicate this book to my Lord and Savior, Jesus Christ, for helping me discover my uniqueness. To the memory of my father and mother, Gene McDaniel and Lorraine Bunton.

I also dedicate this book to Glen White, my loving husband, and my three angels here on earth, my children Michael, David, and Gabrielle White. I could not have achieved this book without your unwavering support throughout the completion of this project. And to my niece, Christina Hammond.

DISCOVERING YOUR UNIQUENESS

I was born with Uniqueness; I will not be denied
I am deeply motivated filled with unwavering self-pride
I swim with sharks and walk with strong lions
I am fully capable of climbing Mount Zion
I will never be a sheep, following along as I go
I soar high with the eagles, as the mighty wind blows
I will stay focused on my Uniqueness and never give up
My goal is to overflow my success-driven cup
I will not allow roadblocks or setbacks to bog me down
Because of my Uniqueness, I wear my success crown
I am not a lazy cow, grazing in the pastures all-day
I am speedy like the roadrunner, fast on my way
If you want to succeed, remember this clue
Discovering Your Uniqueness will most certainly assist you

-Michael Bart Mathews ©

ACKNOWLEDGMENTS

A special thank you to our team at Skyward Books, Michael White, for your Uniqueness in bringing the cover design into reality.

I also want to thank Michael and Robbie Mathews of The Mathews Entrepreneur Group – USA. You both have supported and helped me in pursuit of this project.

ACKNOWLEDGEMENTS

INTRODUCTION

Uniqueness is the quality of being one of its kind – exceptional, rare, or incomparable. This book will help you acknowledge and embrace your uniqueness by reflecting on what being unique means to you. Your uniqueness is what makes you special and one of a kind. Your uniqueness is your secret sauce for transformation, change, achievement, and service to others.

Whether you are an actor, lawyer, teacher, musician, or entrepreneur, being unique is what sets you apart. Your uniqueness is within you, from your thoughts, beliefs, behaviors, and the content of your character.

We are all fearfully and wonderfully made! As we grow older, we develop learned behaviors from our ongoing, never-ending life experiences.

Earl Nightingale – "We become what we think about." Thinking is precisely what this book is about. I take you on an ebb and flow journey of introspection of Discovering Your Uniqueness. This book is a challenge of your own mental and emotional process of how you think, feel, and act within the paradigms of your uniqueness. Yes, you will read a touch of spirituality, mixed in with the everyday walks of life that we endure.

While you pursue life, liberty, and the pursuit of happiness, you now hold in your hands a roadmap filled with guideposts to assist you along your journey. Discovering Your Uniqueness can be found in every chapter throughout this book. It is my sincere gratitude that you Discover Your Uniqueness within the pages of this book. Happy reading!

CHAPTER 1

Don't Abandon Your Uniqueness

The definition of uniqueness is the quality of being only one of its kind. The quality of being particularly remarkable, extraordinary, exceptional. Psalm 139:14 – "That we are fearfully and wonderfully made, marvelous are the works and that my soul knoweth right well."

Psalm 139:15 – "My substance was not hide from Thee, when I was made in secret, and curiously wrought in the lowest parts of the earth."

Psalm 139:16 – "Thine eyes did see my substance, yet being unperfect, and in Thy book all my members when written, which in continuance, were fashioned, when as yet there was none of them."

God knows every person from the womb to the tomb. God knows you are unique because He formed you in your mother's womb. God knows the precise knowledge about your life down to the nanosecond of when you will be born into the world and leaving this world. He understands the choices you will make throughout your life.

Each of us has a unique spirit soul that is encapsulated

inside of our unique and wonderfully made bodies. Since we are made in the image and likeness of God as He says in Genesis 1:26 – "Let Us make man in our image, after Our likeness and let them have dominion over the fish of the sea and over the fowl of the air, and over the cattle, and overall the earth, and over every creeping thing that creepeth upon the earth."

Genesis 1:27 – "So God created man in his own image, in the image of God created them; male and female created He them." God governs all things from creation to the cosmos, like the birds, the bees, the flowers, and the trees. The planets, the moon, the stars, the constellations. Even the sun, the wind, the rain are creations of God. Including Adam & Eve and every descendant.

He created everything throughout our seamlessly never-ending universe and filled the earth with all the resources needed for humanity not just to survive but to strive.

You are not a mistake. You have a purpose and reason for being here. Maybe you were born out of wedlock or adopted and did not know your birth parents. Either way, you were not created by the Heavenly Father and birthed from your earthly mother by mistake. The mistake is when we go to our grave, not knowing our WHY- our REASON - or our PURPOSE for living.

Many people struggle with how they think, act, and feel about life, liberty, and the pursuit of happiness. Their outward appearance suffers from inward feelings of inadequacy about their experience. By discovering your uniqueness and building upon your abilities, you can make the paradigm shift that will allow you to discover your uniqueness.

You are a masterpiece because you are a piece of the master. We were all born unique and wonderfully made! More often than not, the vast majority of people are buried in a graveyard without fulfilling their dreams.

Les Brown – "The graveyard is the richest place on earth because it is here that you will find all those hopes and dreams that were never fulfilled, the books that were never written, the songs that were never sung, the inventions that were never shared, the cures that were never discovered, all because someone was too afraid to TAKE THE FIRST STEP, keep with the problem, or determined to carry out their dream."

Do not become one of those unique and wonderfully made people who walk around being a wandering generality. We all can become a meaningful specific and share our gifts with the world once we discover our WHY. Then we can harness the power of purpose!

I admire people who have special needs or a disability because many go beyond their limitations and live full lives. There are many stories where someone with a disability has persevered through adversity, trials & tribulations. While discovering their uniqueness, they found their seeds of greatness, despite their everyday, ongoing life challenges.

Some of these people may be without arms or legs like Unstoppable Tracy Schmitt/a quadruple amputee. Or without vision, like Helen Keller, Ray Charles & Stevie Wonder. Or without hearing, like Ludwig van Beethoven, Thomas Edison, and Helen Keller! The list could go on and on and include thousands of every day, not so famous people with special needs and disabilities.

Using the above examples, why are there so many able body people who never accomplish half as much as those brave souls who have disabilities?

Our world is full of unique people, places, and things that God has made. There is uniqueness in birth, colors, animals, scenery, sounds, food, ideas, lifestyles, spiritual beliefs, etc. We all have in common our human characteristics because we are all made in God's image.

We are all a unique and wonderfully made limited edition. We have our own special trademark from birth. The National Forensic Science Technology Center states, "no two people have ever been found to have the same fingerprints – including identical twins." Also, the fingerprints on our hands each have a UNIQUE print. This theory has been debated about the pros and cons of its validity; however, the fact remains, we are unique. We are all unlike no other!

Think about your unique social security number. The purpose was designed to track your earnings history and determine your social security benefits. Like your fingerprints, the retina in your eyes, and yes, your social security number, they are all unique unto you.

God wants to accomplish something in you and through you that the world can benefit. Many people were given a combination of gifts or talents given by God. If we choose to accept it, our mission is to find our real purpose and share it with the world so that others can benefit from our blessings.

Matthew 25:15 – (paraphrased) "And unto one, he gave five talents, to another two, and to another one, to every man according to his several ability." A talent is a natural aptitude or skill. As stated in Matthew 25:15 above, God gave different people different amounts of talents and abilities. He left no one out!

You were not manufactured on an assembly line. You were individually fearfully and wonderfully made with your own UNIQUENESS! God has a plan for all His creations, and we are His Creation.

Jeremiah 29:11,13 – "For I know the thoughts that I think towards you sayeth the Lord, thoughts of peace and not of evil to give you an expected end."

Jeremiah 29:13 – "And ye shall seek me when ye shall search for me with all your heart."

Do not let your uniqueness stay buried inside of you and paralyze what you can offer the world. God has not given us the spirit of fear! F.E.A.R. is a learned belief and behavior.

God has given us the power of love, the ability to think, and the power to overcome our F.E.A.R!

You are a powerhouse; you are at the top of God's creation. The world is waiting for you to discover your gifts so you can serve the needs of the people. The universe will make room for you to bring your gifts before great men.

When you talk to yourself and say things like; I am tired, I am bored, I am nothing, I am dumb, I can't succeed, or this is too hard, you are speaking prophetically or foretelling your future failures.

Dr. James Dentley III – "When you change the way you look at things, the things you look at change."

Your words have power. Remember earlier when we talked about having dominion over the earth and everything in it. Being like our Creator, He spoke everything into existence in the book of Genesis.

We have naming power that can be both right and wrong or good or evil. You must be conscious of your words. Do not get hung by your tongue. Be careful about the words that come out of our mouths.

We can speak things into existence, and so it will appear. However, having faith without works is dead. Jesus spoke positive affirmations over His life. He said things like I am the way I am the living water, I am the door, I am the resurrection and life, I am the good shepherd. Jesus understood his uniqueness, so His habits and His words were in sync with who He was and what he wanted to accomplish.

When we understand that big U on our chest that represents our uniqueness, we have that same ability to accomplish our burning desires in life. When we use spiritual affirmations such as Matthew 7:7 – "Ask, and it shall be given unto you; seek, and ye shall find; knock and it shall be opened unto you." Our responsibility is to take action after asking for God's blessings and guidance over that which we seek!

His prayer life shaped His future for His destiny. Working with your gifts and talents and stepping up to life's challenges helps you respond like a superhero. A superhero possesses talents and skills far beyond the average, everyday, ordinary person. These are the kind of people who are not afraid to let the letters on their chest shine. The U for uniqueness on your chest is there to build the framework for you to activate your talents and skills, providing tremendous results.

You have it in you to map out and discover your uniqueness. Our imagination is an incredible force that can create new paths and turn the impossible into possible achievements. When used with purpose and intention, you can help make this world a better place.

Activating your talents and gifts can be the difference between living a mediocre, an ordinary, or an extraordinary life.

The MEDIOCRE life is the one that wants you to abandon your uniqueness. It gives you thoughts like, you are below average, you will fail. You do not have enough education, talent, or skills; you are not good enough. They are not at all in the game!

ORDINARY life is being average or acting like sheep. Everyone follows the leader. They all live the same lifestyle, never advancing beyond the 40-40-40 plan, meaning working 40 hours per week, for 40 years of your life, to retire on 40 percent of your income! They are in the game, but they are not your game-changers.

EXTRAORDINARY is above average, like living the life of a superhero. You found your moment of clarity. You know WHY you are here on earth. You embrace the U on your chest. You found your passion and are making it happen as you serve the needs of others and your family. They are leaving a legacy. They are your game changers!

You must be willing to fire up your faith and not listen to your fears.

Let us talk about the meaning of F.E.A.R. The old school definition of F.E.A.R. means, False Evidence Appearing Real. I'm sure you've heard that analogy before. The new school definition of F.E.A.R. means; "Feeling Excited And Ready."

People who Feel Excited And Ready are usually those eager souls who are living a purpose-driven life. They know their WHY. Before the birds start tweeting, they get up early before the sun rises, before the average person drags him or herself out of bed, dreading the life they live, yet they fail to do anything about it.

On the other hand, the extraordinary life has a mindset that says I am, I can, and I will accomplish my goals. Use positive statements or affirmations to encourage, motivate, and inspire you along your way. Practice on a small scale, doing what you love because you love what you do. There is a better best inside of you waiting to break free. Once you identify that better best in you, you can surely bet that there are better days ahead.

Do not give up on yourself. Do not give up on your dreams. My daughter says; "When relying on society's stereotypes to be your standard, telling you who you are, who you are going to be, and all you will ever become, you will miss the mark and reality of the totality of your potential purpose and stone written promises of God for yourself."

Understanding and discovering our uniqueness by consulting with God through prayer and meditation is a must-have. We have a direct line to God using prayer. God is on speed dial because all we must do is simply Pray. It is in those quiet times that God can bring about a radical change. A changed point of view and spiritual unfoldment. This change can benefit individuals seeking more truth and light. They can discover more about who they are and what their purpose in life is.

Prayer can bring about the ability to make good sound judgments of righteousness, over and beyond the wickedness surrounding our lives. Prayer can disrupt your current way of thinking about yourself and give you a fresh, new outlook on things. Prayer can help you to gain the courage to dream. Faith can help you cast your vision. Action can deliver the dreams that you seek to obtain in life. Prayer can help change the canvas of your life. Faith can help you paint an entirely new picture that is surrounding the current frame of your life.

The bible says to pray without ceasing. I think this means to consult with God about more of our daily decisions. God wants a personal relationship with us, not just on weekends at church. Your gift will make room for you and bring you before great men.

Develop your character, embrace your talent, practice your skillset, read, learn, and sharpen your iron. Proverbs 27:17 – "As iron sharpens iron, so one person sharpens another." There is a saying that says if you want to earn more, learn more. Align yourself with principles that will help you excel. The power of believing in your abilities allows you to show up and be deliberate and intentional towards your goals.

Do not abandon your uniqueness. What do I mean by this? Well, let's look at what abandonment feels like to a certain degree. Abandonment can make you feel undesirable to yourself. Abandonment can cause you to feel lonely, left behind, insecure, or discarded.

People in this state can often feel lost or cut off from mainstream society. They do not receive the crucial resources needed to live an everyday life filled with sustenance. They become distant and further withdrawn from society.

Children left at adoption agencies, given away at birth, or in the foster care system might develop abandonment feelings once they get older. True enough, the families that raised them, in most cases, gave them love and a happy home. Once they learned about being abandoned, unless you are in one of the categories mentioned above, one never truly knows its impact on their thought process. Even an adult that has gone through a divorce might develop feelings of abandonment. Abandonment leaves you with feelings of discouragement, discontent, weariness, and failure.

The aftereffects of abandonment can sometimes cause a person to push back from others to avoid rejection socially. Abandonment can leave one with a feeling of codependency. It can also cause a person to give up too much in a relationship or always wanting to be a people pleaser.

I felt abandoned when my parents divorced when I was a child. I did not understand all the reasons for the breakdown in their marriage and overall relationship. I did have the feeling of abandonment from my father not being around anymore. Years later, as an adult, I realized those feelings were deep-rooted inside my thoughts and feelings.

Understanding my feelings of abandonment finally helped me live a fuller life and not blame myself or anyone else for the erosion of my parent's marriage.

Ironically, when my father died, and years later, when my mother died, I found myself resurfacing those thoughts and feelings of abandonment. It seemed like I was an orphan without my mom and dad here on earth with me. I had lots of family and siblings that helped me through that difficult time. I can relate to abandonment issues due to my own experience.

The Serenity Prayer is an empowering spiritually related; personal development tool to strengthen your resolve with abandonment issues and other issues or challenges in your life.

The Serenity Prayer is a widely used affirmation when things in your life go wrong, as they sometimes will. During this time is when we "Trust in the Lord with all thine heart; and lean not unto thine own understand." By praying or merely stating the Serenity Prayer, we are leaning on God to shine the light of understanding upon us.

"God, grant me the serenity to accept the things that I cannot change, courage to change the things I can, and the wisdom to know the difference." – Reinhold Niebuhr.

The Serenity Prayer is in Isaiah 41. I encourage you to pick up the Good Book and read it in its entirety. Remember – readers are leaders!

Let's get back to our fireside chat about abandonment. A circumstance in life that could have occurred that was not your fault could have caused abandonment issues. Abandonment issues can also happen in the workplace, in relationships, even within your own family and your social environment.

I think one of the worst abandonment feelings is when people feel God has abandonment them. This feeling of abandonment makes one feels that God has forsaken you. Often, we do not know God's plan for our lives. God is ahead of us in His plan for our lives. God's word says in Jeremiah 29:11 – "For I know the thoughts that I think towards you, saith the Lord, thoughts of peace, and not of evil, to give you an expected end."

The more we develop a closer relationship with God, the more we will see that He is faithful and will not forsake or abandon us. God is there through the storms of life and in the calm. God has His will and His timing.

Sometimes testing, setback, roadblocks, speedbumps, and even failure build character. We do not have to have a rollercoaster of emotions when it comes to trusting God. Romans 8:28 – "And we know that all things work together for good to those who love God, and to those who are called according to His purpose." Matthew 28:20 – "And behold I am with you always, even to the end of the age."

God will not abandon us, and He does not want us to dismiss our gifts, talents, and uniqueness that He has given us. Even when we stumble and fall, God is there to pick us up. Psalm 46:1 – "God is a very present help in times of trouble."

In the book of Daniel, Shadrach, Meshach, and Abednego, three Hebrews men were thrown into a fiery furnace by King Nebuchadnezzar of Babylon when they refused to bow down to the king's image. The three were protected from harm, and the king sees four men walking in flames, the fourth like the Son of God. God is a present help in times of need.

God is there to help us physically, emotionally, and spiritually. Those three men had to embrace their uniqueness, separate from the others, by not bowing down on that faithful day.

Think about the story of Rudolph, the red nose reindeer. A Christmas favorite among children. Rudolph's special feature (his red nose) made him UNIQUE from the other reindeers. At first, Rudolph tried to abandon his uniqueness and fit in with all the other reindeers.

Santa did not allow that to happen. Why, because Santa saw the uniqueness in Rudolph. He asked Rudolph the following question on one foggy Christmas eve, "Rudolph with your nose so bright, won't you guide my sleigh tonight?"

Because Santa saw in Rudolph, what Rudolph did not first see in himself, his unique red nose was a beacon of light on that foggy Christmas eve. Rudolph became a leader instead of a follower because he embraced the light from his distinctive red nose. Embrace your light and uniqueness and become the leader, not the follower.

As we briefly discussed earlier, the world has enough volunteers who are living average or mediocre lives. Many imitators try to live off someone else's uniqueness, talents, or gifts instead of showing the world their exceptional, unique capabilities.

Singer Judy Garland said, "Always be a first-rate version of yourself and not a second-rate version of someone else." Years ago, many young boys wanted to be like Michael Jordan, the Chicago Bulls six-time NBA world championship basketball player. There was a phrase "be like Mike" going around. No one was ever able to match his gift and talents in that era of basketball.

Let's get back to Rudolph. He decided not to abandon his uniqueness, and in that story, he saved Christmas. How many people can you save by Discovering Your Uniqueness?

Do not spend time trying to fit in. Your time can be more useful in discovering your uniqueness, talents, and gifts. You may not go down in history as a hero or shero, but your light will shine before those you are serving. Live out your uniqueness! Let go of any restraints that are holding you back from living your purpose-driven life. Your life will take on an entirely new meaning and direction when you do not abandon your uniqueness.

You are unique and wonderfully made because you are

God's creation. You are so unique that an internet source states that a healthy adult male can release about 40 million to 1.2 billion sperm cells during a single ejaculation during the reproductive process.

It takes about 24-hours for a sperm cell to fertilize an egg. The one individual sperm that fertilized the one unique egg, in a field of over 2-million other competing eggs, brought one unique person into this world. And that person is YOU!

You survived the unique birth process because all other sperm cells disintegrate because they cannot fertilize an egg.

You may have things in common with other family members, such as looks or behaviors, but you are still one of a kind. Your fingerprints (as discussed earlier), your voice, and genetic (DNA) makeup are unique to you. Since God is extraordinary, He included the gift of uniqueness into every person. We need to understand our value on this earth.

God made you, and He does not make junk! Many people may struggle with personal issues like their appearance, low self-esteem, lack of education, and feelings of inadequacy.

But if they embrace their uniqueness and build upon their ability, their chances of being more outgoing and successful in life are more significant. You are one of a kind.

Scientists say that the chances of two snowflakes being exactly alike are one in one million trillion. That is one, followed by eighteen zeros. Meteorologists think that there are one trillion, trillion, trillion types of snowflakes. That is one, followed by thirty-six zeros. Remember, we are like snowflakes, all different and unique from our creator.

Just like our gifts and talents, everyone has within them 'that special something.' We must dig down deep within our mind, body, and soul and discover our uniqueness before we can share it with the world.

SHEILA THOUGHTS

THINGS THAT MAKE YOU GO HMMMM

1. Start where you are today!

2. Think about things you are already doing that you are good at, regardless of pay.

3. Think about and choose the Uniqueness of the qualities needed for you to be effective.

4. Now, list the unique qualities that you have discovered about yourself?

5. Would you agree that your Uniqueness comes from your passion and desire while you are moving forward?

6. What are some ways that your uniqueness can serve and help others?

7. What are some talents and gifts you can celebrate about yourself?

8. What can you do today to start walking in your Uniqueness?

9. Who can you help to find their uniqueness?

10. Would you agree that your Uniqueness operates out of your mission and value statement about yourself?

CHAPTER 2

Something More "A State Of Mind"

We live in a day and a time when most people want more. People want more time, more money, more houses, more cars, more clothes, more technology. It seems everywhere you turn; people are not content with what they have.

The bible speaks about contentment in Philippians 4:11 – "Not that I speak in respect of want for I have learned in whatsoever state I am, therewith to be content."

It seems like our society lives in a state of discontentment. We are not happy with our children, spouse, jobs, health, environment, leaders, or finances. The list could go on and on and on.

Many are looking for love in the wrong places, trying to fill a void that cannot be satisfied. The reason people fill discontentment is that earthly things cannot fulfill us spiritually.

True contentment is in Jesus Christ. It is not in things, or people, or circumstances. My mother used to say, "We brought nothing into this world, and we can take nothing out of it."

I have seen people wearing beautiful jewelry in their casket at their funeral. On one occasion, a young man was seated in a special made, custom casket, built like a car. I have never seen an armored car full of money & personal possessions following behind a funeral procession. You cannot take it with you to your grave!

In America, we take the abundance of available freedoms that third-world countries do not have access for granted. The United States is a country of opportunity for everyone. As stated in the Star-Spangled Banner, "The Land of the Free and the Home of the Brave."

At the age of twenty-five, most people are optimistic (hopeful & confident) about life and ready to meet the world head-on. My mom used to say when I was in my twenties; the world is your oyster. My mom meant plenty of opportunities were available for me, even if those opportunities were not out there for her in her youthful days as a young woman.

But after life's bumps and bruises, hills, and valleys, those who make it to age sixty-five often have a different view. A survey says that if you track 100 people starting at age 25, do you have any idea what will happen to those people by the time they reach age 65? And the survey says:

- One will be rich
- Four will be financially independent
- Five will still be working

- Fifty-four will be broke and depending on other's for life's necessities
- Thirty-six will be dead

Only 5 out of 100 become financially independent. Most young men and women in their twenties will most likely tell you that they will be successful later in life. They would have a good, middle-class paying job. They also say they will own their own business, or become an entrepreneur. Maybe they will get married and own a home with a white picket fence while raising a family.

But the reality is, many people will not be successful by the time they reach age 65, according to the previous survey.

One of the main reasons people who reach age 65 and are not financially secure is because of the decisions and choices they made. Most people make one deadly choice "they fail to plan, so they plan to fail." By taking little to no action toward achievement, you are conforming outside of working for someone else.

Falling into conformity can be a problem. My mom used to say about some people is that all they wanted in life was a boot and a shoe. She meant they did not want much out of life. Conformity can be a disaster for uniqueness. They were conforming to merely surviving as their low-aim goal. The problem is when you reach that low-aim goal; you are worst off than ever before!

Living just enough for the city is not just enough,

Financially Speaking. Because of conformity, many people have not learned how to be financially successful in one of the riches lands that we have ever known. God does not want us to conform to this world! We must change how we think, feel, and act by renewing our minds.

People's lives can be influenced by their environment or by what happens to them. How many times have you heard of or read about someone succeeding despite unfavorable circumstances when faced with adversity? Instead of having low-aim goals, every successful person has high-aim plans for reaching their goals.

Most people do things because everyone else is doing it. If you walk down the street and stop at the corner and look up into the sky, chances are, other people will stop and lookup. Why? Because people conform to automatic behavior patterns without realizing they have developed this habit. People will imagine they see something even if it's just a funny shaped cloud.

Why do some people work hard in life and seem to end up with very little? Why and how do others work less and end up with more? I believe that people with goals and action plans for success seem to advance more.

People with goals tend to get more out of life and seem to live a more fulfilled life. Habakkuk 2:2 – "And the Lord answered me and said, write the vision, and make it plain upon tables, that he may run that readeth it."

Having goals and working towards achievement is what

I call a plan. We all want more but are we willing to work towards our goals? We all need coaching and guidance! We should not go through life like a ship without a rudder, no engine, or crew to man the sails. We need S.M.A.R.T. goals.

We all can benefit from using the S.M.A.R.T. Goal System below.

- **S**pecific – Cleary write down your goals. Identify who, besides yourself, is responsible for achieving said goals.
- **M**easurable – How many, how much, and how often must you indulge until you achieve your goals.
- **A**chievable - Is a fixed date of achievement attached to your goals? Do you have all the resources needed for achievement, and are the expected results realistic?
- **R**elevant – Will your goal make a difference in your personal life? In your business Life? In the lives of others?
- **T**imebound – Did you begin with the end in mind? Meaning, does your goal have a specific ending date of accomplishment?

We become what we think about! The bible says – "As a man thinketh in his heart so is he." – Proverbs 27:7. In other words, what you think about you bring about, good, bad, or indifferent. We used to call my mom boss, and as she used to say – "Use your head for more than a hat rack."

Ralph Waldo Emerson — "A man is what he thinks about, all day long." William James — "If you only care for a result, you will almost certainly attain it. If you want to be rich, you will attain it. If you wish to be a scholar, you can attain it. If you wish to be good, you can attain it. Only wish these exclusively, and not wish a hundred other incompatible things just as strongly."

Mark 9:23 — "Jesus said unto him, If thou can believe, all things are possible to him that believeth." If you think negative thoughts, you reap negative results. If you think positive thoughts, you reap positive results. We become what we think about! Napoleon Hill — "Whatever the mind of man can conceive and believe, it can achieve."

If you want something more in life, write down your S.M.A.R.T. goals and write down your plan for success. Add your date of accomplishment! Now, use the speed of implementation by taking action and working your plan. Benjamin Franklin — "If you fail to plan, you plan to fail."

Nothing comes to a sleeper but a dream. A dream without a plan is like having faith without works. Rev. Dr. Johnnie Coleman was a very influential African American minister and teacher of the New Thought Movement, based out of Chicago. One of her favorite sayings was — "I am the thinker that thinks the thoughts that make the things."

If you think about nothing, you become nothing. The mind does not care about what you put in it because it always returns what you plant. The bible says as you sow, so shall you reap. The mind is free at birth. The ways of the world taint our thoughts. As we grow older, we experience growing pains from life's many teachable moments.

People place too much emphasis on things that cost more money than they can afford to spend. Many people suffer from shiny object syndrome by putting their wants ahead of their needs! Things like luxury homes, expensive cars, designer clothes, jewelry, and vacations are paid for by credit cards. Now they are deep in debt.

If you can afford the shiny objects, enjoy them. I am talking to the person who tries to keep up with the Joneses while living on a bean dip and shoestring budget.

Things like our souls, hopes, dreams, ambitions, and families are priceless. The shiny objects that cost a lot of money are cheap compared to the value placed on our souls and loved ones. Shiny objects can always be replaced, but not our loved ones. We are the sum total of our thoughts.

The mind contains riches beyond our wildest dreams. Scientists say we are using only ten percent of our brainpower. We use our minds frequently for little jobs instead of big important ones. We are guided by the thoughts that we think; whether our ideas are good, bad, right, or wrong, we must control our thinking. Our minds should be pure and positive. Not the open-door garbage disposal filled with doubt, fear, and negativity.

People use their minds for the good, the bad, and the

ugly. Ask yourself, am I willing to pay the price to improve my life and the life of my children's children?

For things to change, you must be willing to change. For things to get better, you must get better. Goals are accomplished first in the mind, then transformed into reality.

Do not entrust your future to anyone who does not share your values, goals, and dreams. There is tremendous power in discovering your uniqueness. The bible says in Proverbs 18:16 – "A man's gift makes room for him." There is a gift inside of you, and the world will make room for you.

It is not just your education; the secret sauce is your gift. People will pay you for your gift. Your unique gift is your key to success. Choose something that will enhance your unique skill and talent. Adopting the 5-hour rule principles is a good starting point that will help you develop your gift!

The 5-hour rule, which Michael Simmons states: "No matter how busy, successful people are, they always spend at least an hour a day – or five hours (minimum) a week – learning or practicing."

Know that God has something more in store for you. Do not believe God wants you to live a life of pain and struggle. God wants us all to live a life of meaning. Our thoughts, choices, and actions matter. Fulfillment comes from doing rewarding, meaningful, and purposeful things.

Prayer helps give you wisdom and direction. James 1:5 – "If any of you lacks wisdom, let him ask God who gives generously to all without reproach, and it will be given him." Read God's word to find your purpose. God speaks to us through the bible. Psalm 119:105 – "Your word is a lamp unto my feet and a light unto my path."

The bible tells us that Jesus will keep us in perfect peace because we trust in Him. It is essential to feed our minds with good thoughts. Our thoughts can help transform our lives. Bob Proctor – "Thoughts become things. If you see it in your mind, you can hold it in your hand."

Confucius – "The more man meditates upon good thought, the better will be his world and the world at large."

Marcus Aurelius – "You have power over your mind, not outside events."

The mind is a terrible thing to waste! It is especially important because this is how the spirit of God communicates with us. The mind can affect our thinking, allowing us to act upon those thoughts in many ways. Man can be inspired or discouraged by his thoughts.

You can ascend in life by harnessing the power of your positive thoughts. And you can descend in life by allowing the negative influence of thought to rule your mind. Do not let your mind run wild, root out the toxic thinking that does not serve you.

Zig Ziglar – "Feed your mind with the good, the clean, the pure, the powerful, and the positive." Bad thoughts produce bad fruit. Good thoughts produce good fruit. The miracle power of thinking takes place in the mind.

These things can help you move forward or keep you where you are. The mind can help you feel powerful or powerless. Before you transition and depart from this life, decide to live your purpose-driven, best life to the fullest! Leave a positive contribution to society.

Once God launches your internal guiding system of positive thoughts, you can accelerate your S.M.A.R.T. goals. You will be well on your way to achieving your heart's burning desire. When defining your S.M.A.R.T. goals, always remember to be Specific, Measurable, Attainable, Relevant, and Time-based within your written outline.

SHEILATHOUGHTS
THINGS THAT MAKE YOU GO HMMMM

1. Write down that 'special something' that you want most in life.

2. Before you go to sleep at night, write down your goals for the next day.

3. What sacrifices are you willing to make to accomplish your goals?

4. At the end of the next day, review how many goals on your list did you accomplish.

5. Any goals that you did not accomplish determine what held you back.

6. In the next twelve months, I will accomplish _____.

7. In the next twenty-four months, I will accomplish _____.

8. In the next five years, I will accomplish_____.

9. In the next ten years, I will accomplish_____.

10. What will my legacy be for my children and my children's children? What impact will my legacy have on the world?

CHAPTER 3

Assurance Not Insurance

In this world, almost everything has a price. According to the National Association of Insurance Commissioners, in 2018, there were 5,965 insurance companies in the United States. Insurance company products include life and annuities, health, risk retention groups, and other products. The insurance industry has grown significantly with a vast number of diversified products to serve consumers' needs.

People buy insurance for many different reasons. For instance, if you own a home, the mortgage lending institution requires you to purchase protection in the form of homeowner's insurance. People also buy health insurance to offset the skyrocketing health care costs of hospital stay, prescription drugs, dental, and vision care.

Long-term care insurance is another instrument people purchase to cover medical expenses in their elder years, like short or long-term nursing home care or in-home doctor visits.

Insurance is a way of managing financial risk while providing products and services that fits your needs. Some companies offer group benefits and retirement options for employees. Yes, insurance can be expensive, and yes, insurance is needed!

Many people do not have insurance because they cannot afford to pay the premiums. A medical emergency can cause you to go bankrupt. Having insurance is not a luxury. It is a necessity. Allow me to share the following short story with you.

My husband and I once owned two vehicles, a newer model and an older model. We paid full coverage on the new model and liability on the older model. After being involved in an accident with the older vehicle, we could not replace it because our liability insurance coverage helps pay for the cost of the other drivers' property (not our car) and medical injuries/expenses if you are deemed "at fault."

I felt anger when the insurance agent explained there was nothing he could do. In short, we were paying more money every month on the older vehicle. Our agent told us that we were underinsured.

Disappointed and angered, we switched insurance companies to a carrier that we had before. We initially paid a lower price, but it did not work out for us in the end. Using my story as an example, before purchasing any insurance, make sure you understand the coverage options.

Some excellent insurance agents will provide you with all the information needed while helping you make sound decisions. They take their fiduciary oath seriously! On the other hand, some agents focus on selling you products that you do not need to line their pockets. You don't know until you don't know!

The word assurance means a positive declaration intended to give confidence, a promise, certainty about something. Understanding the word assurance brings me to a point about Jesus Christ. We can have the assurance that we belong to him. Because of Jesus, we are heirs to salvation! He purchased our salvation by dying on the cross for our sins instead of us dying for our sins.

God has given us something more dependable than insurance, He has given us His son Jesus Christ, which is our assurance. It says in His word that if we trust in Him, all our sins will be forgiven. 1 John 5:13 – "These things have I written unto you that believe on the name of the Son of God, that ye may know that ye have eternal life and that ye may believe on the name of the son of God."

The name Jesus is a name that is greater than any other name. You can have assurance in Jesus' name. In the name of Jesus, if a man or woman is sick, they can get well. In the name of Jesus, a man or woman is unlearned; they can find wisdom. A bad or evil man or woman can become virtuous.

Even a dead man can be resurrected and brought back to life. It is because of the name of Jesus. Our assurance, unlike insurance, is what we have in Jesus.

Jesus said that He would be with us even to the ends of the earth! God owns everything, all the cattle on a thousand hills are His, and the hills are His real estate. He does not have to copyright the songs that He puts in the birds, nor does God have to trademark His name on the canopy of the beautiful blue sky because He owns it.

We can have assurance in Jesus Christ because He came down from heaven and was born in Bethlehem of a virgin mother, later moving with his family to live in Nazareth. Mary, Joseph, and Jesus fled to Egypt to escape Herod the Great's slaughter of Bethlehem's baby boys. Jesus was baptized in the River Jordan by his cousin, John the Baptist.

Jesus performed many miracles on hills and mountains. He spoke to the multitude by the wayside. He healed thousands without medicine and did not charge for his services. Jesus conquered every obstacle that came against him, even being led by the Spirit into the wilderness to be tempted by the devil, who was trying to rob him of his assurance in God.

He hung on the cross and bled to His death for our sins.

Even though Jesus was king of kings, he was buried in a borrowed tomb by a friend who took on the responsibility after the crucifixion. He got right up on time as He promised, and he came back to receive His children right on schedule. As the angels said to the disciples after the ascension of Jesus, why stand ye gazing up into heaven?

The same Jesus ascended into heaven, shall so come in like manner as ye have seen him go up into heaven. Acts 1:11 – "No one can separate you from the love of God."

Even if you do not live up to your fullest potential here on earth, you can not be separated from the love that God has for you.

Romans 8:38,39 – "For I am persuaded, that neither death, nor life, nor angels, nor principality, nor powers, nor things present, nor things to come, nor height, nor depth, nor any other creature shall be able to separate us from the love of God, which is in Christ Jesus our Lord." "God's word is lamp unto our feet and a light unto our path." This, my friends, is true assurance.

SHEILATHOUGHTS

THINGS THAT MAKE YOU GO HMMMM

1. Have you written your (assurance statement) or positive declaration to give your promise to use your abilities for the greater good of humanity?

2. What are some assurances that you believe the bible has for you?

3. What limiting beliefs are holding you back from having full assurance in Jesus' promises.

4. Do you have full assurance in your beliefs that the things you pray about will come about?

5. What actions can you take to help further your belief?

6. Is your faith in Jesus stronger than your fear of worldly events?

7. Is your spiritual belief and assurance strong enough for you to see God's light upon your path?

8. Are you free from doubt that you will walk with the assurance of success?

9. Do you have a strong enough assurance that you have surrounded yourself with the best quality of like-minded people?

10. Do you always think with the assurance that doing right or good deeds is better than doing evil deeds, even when pressured to do wrong by wrongdoers?

CHAPTER 4

Purpose Or Passion

If we do not know our purpose or our reason for being here on earth, we will suffer from our ignorance of God's significance and the pursuit of our everyday life. There are days, weeks, months, and years that keep passing by with people still searching for their purpose or passion in life. Some people look in many of the wrong places and faces, trying to find love, peace, happiness, and financial prosperity.

Looking into the wrong places and faces can lead you down a destructive path. There is no real substitute for the love, joy, and peace that Christ can give. People become addicted to drugs, alcohol, and many other vices, trying to fit into the click or in-crowd.

Addiction gives people a false system of belief. Sometimes they begin feeling braver or more courageous in areas of life. Some, not all performing artists/musicians, have confessed to getting high on drugs before performing live on stage. They appear to take on a different persona or alter-ego from the reactions of their drug usage. Drugs affect people differently. Some performers act more excited, wild, and out of control. In comparison, others behave more relaxed, cool, calm, and collective. Either case, in their minds, the drugs helps them perform better or become more creative.

Many people go to their graves, never really discovering their uniqueness and why they are here on earth. Discovering our uniqueness is the high-octane fuel that feeds our purpose. God knows our real purpose and the reason we came into this world. We were not meant to be just a twinkle in our parents' eyes as a baby. Even if you were not wanted as a baby or welcomed as an additional child on the family tree, you still have a reason for being here on earth. You are not just a survivor; you are a thriver! Being in 'thriver mode' is being in the right mental, physical, emotional, and spiritual environment to flourish.

We do not have to live in the quiet desperation of not realizing that there is more to life than just existing day-to-day. Life has a full meaning, with exploration being at the forefront of advancement. There are many experiences to receive out of life. You do not have to be a world traveler to experience some of life's greatness.

Some experiences can leave you exhilarated and overly excited. Some of those experiences might include tasting different foods, experiencing different cultures, visiting museums, art galleries, state parks, or going to the zoo. You can experience joy in developing a new hobby (write your book), learning a new language, or different music types. The list can go on and on.

Other experiences can leave you distrustful, confused, disturbed, heartbroken, and in total disbelief. Like some of the current events while writing this book. Police brutality, COVID-19, voter suppression, and political discourse, for example. If you see something, say something!

I once heard a story about a man who died and went to heaven. When he arrived, an angel greeted him. The angel showed him around paradise, and he was in awe of how beautiful it was.

Then the angel took him to a building with lots of doors and rooms. The man looked at all the beautiful decor and said, "wow, this is a lot of splendor." The angel took him down the hall to a door that had his name on it. The man asked if he could go into the room. The angel said yes, and quietly escorted him in.

Once inside, the man could see that God filled the room with different size gift boxes with his name on them. The boxes had not opened. The man got excited and asked, "are all these gifts, mine?" The angel looked at him and said, "yes, these are all the gifts that were available to you while you were on earth. You never asked for them, so they are still here, never opened.

The man looked astonished! He realized the gifts that he could have enjoyed on earth, that would have made his life and those around him more fulfilled. The man never received those gifts because he never asked.

After reading the following paragraph, STOP for a moment!

First, THINK about the many gifts that God has already delivered to you, whether you asked or not. Now write them down.

Second, THINK about the many gifts you have not asked God for, now write them down.

Third, THINK about how you can best help and serve your family, friends, community, and church after receiving those gifts.

Forth, IMAGINE, how many people's lives can positively affect after receiving the gifts you ask for?

Here is your opportunity to take time out of your schedule (in a prayerful, meditative quiet state of mind) and communicate directly with God. Refer to your list and ask for the gifts that you have not yet asked for. "Ask, and it shall be given to you." "Seek, and ye shall find." Knock and the door shall be open." After you ask for your gifts, do not sit back down and pick up that heavy-weight remote control, and start exercising your fingers by changing channels while watching television all day! Do not become or stay a lazy person – better known as a couch potato.

Couch potato, defined by Merriam-Webster – "A lazy and inactive person, especially: one who spends a great deal of time watching television." Remember, Faith, without works, is dead.

God wants us to use every gift available to us. We should want to use everything God has purposed for us. Sometimes we have not because we asked not. Your gifts are not just for you; they are given to you for others to benefit from your talents. When you do not understand your purpose-driven life and your unique gifts, others suffer in this universe.

The next great cinematographer, writer, artist, scientist, doctor, architect, teacher, or designer are finding their gifts and talents despite the adversities from COVID-19 during this devastating global pandemic in the year 2020. Many creative thinkers are showing the world what they can achieve because of their gifts and talents. They were able to harness the power of purpose, and you have the ability to do the same.

Exodus 9:16 – "And in every deed (purpose) for this cause have I raised thee up, for to shew in thee my power, and that my name may be declared throughout all the earth."

God even had a purpose for those who resisted Him, like Pharaoh in the bible. Pharaoh mistakenly thought he was in control. God showed him at the end of the story that Pharaoh had to let Israel's children go. They were then free to serve God the way they choose.

When God opens a door, no man can shut it. Pharaoh had to follow God's plan and purpose. Pharaoh wore himself out, trying to go against God's plan and purpose for the Israelites.

Proverbs 19:21 – "There are many devices in a man's heart, nevertheless, the counsel of the Lord, that shall stand." In other words, many are the plans in a man's heart, but the Lord's purpose shall prevail. God's purpose has been fulfilled throughout many generations.

We all have a purpose or calling that is part of God's plan. We can discover and learn how to use our purpose-driven life or miss out on our gifts completely. Have you ever had the feeling that you were in the right place at the right time, with the right people doing the right thing? Please understand, finding your moment of clarity, discovering your power within will empower you to harness the power of your purpose.

Prayer is a personal way to connect with God and to help you better understand your purpose. Pay attention to the signs, nudges, and aha-ha moments that seem to come out of thought or thin air! God works mysteriously through our internal guiding system. When we are fully tuned in, tapped in, and turned on to the higher frequency, all things are possible to those who believe!

1 John 5:14 – "And this is the confidence that we have in Him, that if we ask anything in according to His will, he heareth us."

1 John 5:15 – "And if we know that he hears us and

whatever we ask we know what we have the request that we asked of Him."

Another thing we can do is to seek the Godly counsel of an advisor, mentor, or friend that you know, like, and trust. The bible says in a multitude of counselors, there is safety, Proverbs – 11:14. Roman 8:28 – "That all things work together for good to them that love God, to them who are called according to His purpose."

Trust God to lead you where He wants you to go. We do not always do everything correctly, in the right order, or at the right time. But striving to do better is unarguably, still better than just settling for the status quo. The world does not need settlers! The world needs more pioneers, adventurers, and explorers! The world needs every one of us to explore how best we can use our gifts and talents to advance humanity.

Believe you can trust God to guide and lead you to the right resources and the right people to expand your purpose-driven life. Do not let your purpose elude you. Once you fully discover your purpose, your life will never be the same again.

"Beloved, now are we the sons of God, and doth not yet appear what we shall be, but we know that when He shall appear we shall be like Him, for we shall see him as He is" – 1 John 3:2.

Our gifts allow us to perform at a higher level of selflessness by serving and helping others. Once you experience that art of service to others, you will most definitely help change the world.

God wants us to be fruitful in our lives. Discovering your purpose is a pathway to bearing more fruits. Luke 12:48 – "To whom much is given, much will be required! Abide in Me and I in you, as the branch cannot bear fruit of itself except it abide in the vine, no more can ye except ye abide in Me. I Am the Vine; ye are the branches, he that abideth in me and I in Him the same bringeth forth much fruit, for without me ye can do nothing – John 15:4,5. How can you discover your uniqueness and find your purpose? Here are some keys:

- Pray (be specific) to the Father in heaven to help you understand what your purpose is. Focus on and pay attention to your strengths.
- Believe in yourself and your abilities. Remember, Jesus believes in you and ask Him to manifest His virtues in you. Believe that He will manifest his purpose for your life.
- Have confidence that God will answer. Rest in that belief and look to Jesus for victory. Believe He will manifest His virtues and be specific.
- Thank God for the clarity He gives you that will guide your decisions. Remember, you are a masterpiece because you are a piece of the master. Lastly, "Now unto Him that is able to do

exceedingly, abundantly above all that you could ask or think, according to the power that worketh in" − Ephesians 3:20. Reading God's word helps us find our purpose.

God speaks to us through His word. Psalm 119:105 − "Thy word is lamp unto my feet, and a light to my path." God's word throws a beam of light on a dark path. You do not have to swerve an inch off course if you are following God's words. The bright illuminating light from above will direct your path.

Ask yourself whether money was not an issue, what would you be doing in life? You can trust God to lead you where He wants you to go.

Decide that you want God's original plans and purpose for your life. Where no counsel is, the people fall, but there is safety in the multitude of counselors. Seek out the help and advice of others. Do not stop; do not give up. Build your signature lifestyle through your unique gifts and talents. Always strive to understand the purpose and meaning of your life while you are here on earth.

Adopt a winning attitude. Winners never quit, and quitters never win! Repeat the following as often as possible throughout your day; 'If it is to be, it is up to me.' When you look in the mirror of life, you cannot fool or trick the reflection looking back at you.

Your current life is the reflection of how you think,

feel, and act. You get to pick and choose the positive, like-minded actors and the scenes they will play in your everyday life. Life is no dress rehearsal. When the curtain goes up every morning, there no cameras. Your ability to take action is necessary for achievement. You do have the opportunity to write your script (goals). If you do not like it, you can rewrite your life scripts (goals) repeatedly until you get it right.

SHEILATHOUGHTS

THINGS THAT MAKE YOU GO HMMMM

1. What are some known gifts and talents that you can identify about yourself?

2. List your gifts and talents in the order of importance.

3. Identify which of your gifts and talents will have the most significant impact on our society.

4. Identify who your gifts and talents will serve or improve their lives.

5. How can your gifts and talents help and serve others?

6. What are some other areas you would like to explore to enhance your gifts and talents?

7. Identify the driving force behind WHY you will or are using your gifts and talents to serve others.

8. How much extra value, using your gifts and talents, have you, or do you give away for free?

9. How much of your gifts and talents do you charge others for your services?

10. Do you believe that you were born with your own particular unique set of gifts and talents?

CHAPTER 5

Fix Your Focus "Decisions"

In order to Fix Your Focus, you must be willing to make some tough decisions. Not deciding is also a decision. It is essential to understand what options are available. Once your options are clear, your choices can become limitless during the evaluation stage of decision making.

Be willing to admit your mistakes and adjust accordingly. Fix your focus! There is no glory or award for going down the wrong path. As my mother used to say – "Common sense is not so common." I loved her stories and the way she would make sense out of a senseless situation. Another thing she would say was – "When you see crazy coming, cross the street."

When a family member finished working and they walked into my mother's presence, she would say – "You are a skunk lizard." She meant they were stinky and ugly! I laugh today when I think about the narratives that she used. Do not get caught up by paying attention to criticism from other people about your decisions.

The longer the spotlight stays on you in terms of

criticism, that negative energy and attention can become toxic. Activate your positive mental attitude! Map out your life's mission and look for the adventures in your life's calling.

Bet on yourself, adjust your crown, and steady your ladder before you begin to climb. Clarity is the roadmap for success. You can be creating your next move through a well thought out plan of action. Your decisions or lack of decisions can and will impact your destiny and income earning potential.

The phrase" would have, could have, and should have" is a thought and conversation that you do not want to have with yourself in your elder days.

Your decision to act now can lead you to a full range of compatibilities, skills, beliefs, and more talents. Take your warrior stance for your destiny. Fortify your mind and heart against the malicious attacks that will come.

Pray, meditate, read personal development & self-help materials, including the bible. People need the Lord at the end of their broken dreams and goals. God can put the pieces back together.

Break free from any self-destructive, negative habits or patterns. Decide that this will be your season. No more setbacks, no more hold-ups, no more delays. No more settling for, no more status quo, and no more excuses. Do not settle for the un cola when you can have the real cola.

Ask by praying for guidance and peace to operate and

flow freely and abundantly throughout your life. Pray for grace and favor while asking God to deliver unto you the desires of your hearts.

Make the decision and ask for <u>WISDOM,</u> specialized <u>KNOWLEDGE,</u> and <u>UNDERSTANDING</u>! These three words will act as your guideposts along your mental highway of thought, with your destination being accomplishing your goals.

Wisdom is the unique quality of having good, sound judgment based on your knowledge. Have you heard people say that knowledge is power? If knowledge is power, then wisdom is your decision or choice to use or apply that power. You can be wise and knowledgeable at the same time. However, it is safe to say that you cannot be wise without being knowledgeable!

That leaves understanding. Understanding is the ability to understand your knowledge, and the many decisions you make every day. Various internet sources estimate adults make about 35,000 remotely conscious decisions every day. Those same sources say that a child makes about 3,000 decisions every day.

Imagine what can happen once you make the conscious effort to apply the three mental keys 'wisdom, knowledge, and understanding' with every decision you make, every day going forward?

Think about this. Out of the 35,000 decisions you make each day, focus on fixing your thoughts and achieving "that special something" that you desire most in life.

Next, make specific, meaningful, and guided decisions based on your wisdom, knowledge, and understanding of what you want to accomplish.

Once you tie a ribbon around the three keys of success – WISDOM, KNOWLEDGE, AND UNDERSTANDING, the world will become your oyster filled with pearls of priceless, attainable goals.

In the movie Forest Gump, he was asked several times if he was stupid. Forest Gump replied, "Stupid is, as stupid does." Stupid is, as stupid does means, a person should be judge by his/her actions, not by his/her appearance. Using sound wisdom, knowledge, and understanding will surely increase positive results because of taking sound, guided, positive action.

Decide to operate on a higher-level above and beyond the duties of the job. Decide to be diligent, not slothful or lazy. Render more service as unto the Lord and not just to your boss. Decide to lay aside every heavyweight that holds you down from reaching your purpose in life.

Escape the snare of being indecisive. Begin making quick decisions and use the speed of implementation. Decide that you will provide excellent service in what you do. Doing so will allow you to 'attract' the clients you need to grow and scale your business.

Because I use the word 'attract' in the above sentence, let us explore The Law of Attraction being *The Secret* to 'attract' and manifest your heart's desires. The Law of Attraction is the new thought philosophy, not based on scientific ideology. The latest thought process is based on positive thinking!

Rhonda Byrne wrote the book and produced a documentary film, *The Secret*. The movie has high-level interviews with some of the most accomplished and successful Law of Attraction thought leaders and teachers in their area of expertise. From Lisa Nichols, Bob Procter, Joe Vitale, Loral Langemeier, John Assaraf, Jack Canfield, and Michael Bernard Beckwith, among others.

Using the Law of Attraction, *The Secret* is that everyone can create their reality. The driving force is that 'thoughts can become things' are widely discussed throughout the book and movie.

The Law of Attraction states that positive or negative thoughts bring positive or negative experiences into the thinker of those thoughts.

The Law of Attraction, being *The Secret* weapon, can also reflect within your personal life. Remember to under-promise and over-deliver your services to your business partners, your clients, and within your relationships.

The Law of Attraction will allow like-minded people to get to know, like, and trust you on a higher level! As you continue to deliver excellent service, you will attract great customers! Remember, energy is everything, and everything is energy. It takes a certain kind of liked-minded frequency to attract the right type of energy needed for success.

Practice being still while sitting in a quiet place. Clear the cobwebs from your mind while you begin to attract the Holy Spirit. Channel your thoughts and energy in the form of prayer throughout the universe.

Become present and stay tuned in, tapped in, and turned on to the energy and presence of God. This spiritual flow state strengthens your belief and faith that with God, all things are possible.

Proverbs 3:5,6 – "Trust in the Lord with all thine heart and lean not unto thine own understanding. In all thy ways acknowledge Him, and He shall direct thy path."

You do not have to fully understand The Law of Attraction is the *Secret* to manifesting your heart's desire. However, having faith in obtaining that which you seek and taking action toward achievement is what marries The Law of Attraction and *The Secret* together. Having an application of God's word in our lives can lead to a revelation of His will, and we gain strength to carry out His will.

Proverbs – 3:5,6 it teaches us we are not to depend on our own understanding. Instead, we are to trust God for guidance by acknowledging Him by keeping a moment by moment connection with Him through prayer. God is not just concerned with our spiritual decisions. He is also concerned about our choices that affect our everyday lives.

Psalm 32:8 – "I will instruct thee and teach thee in the ways which thou shalt go. I will guide thee with mine eye." Pay attention to what you are consciously thinking. What have you been attracting in your life because of the way you think? Your thoughts do not know when you are joking or being serious. Thoughts immediately begin to grow the positive or negative seeds that you plant in your subconscious mind. The seeds can be good, bad, right, or wrong. The mind will deliver back to you, that which you think.

Earl Nightingale said that we are all self-made, but only the successful will admit it. Nightingale continued, we become what we think about! Messages are continuously transmitted in and out of our minds while we are up and alert and sleeping.

I want to revisit the importance of decisions. We went over this topic earlier. However, I feel it is essential to share a little more in decision-making after talking about the Law of Attraction and *The Secret.*

For our brain to make decisions, it has to choose from at least two processes or courses of action. No, we do not choose or make the right decision all the time. However, when we do make the right decision, we reap the benefits and rewards. Decision making involves choosing between possible solutions to apparent problems. Sometimes the voice of reason makes our sound decisions. Other times, your intuition or feelings will make the decisions.

As stated earlier, we are bombarded with decisions (35,000 for adults & 3,000 for children) all day long. Scientists say we are only using about ten percent of our brainpower. A lot of people allow negative decision making to guide their lives. Then they wonder why they get negative results. They make a decision and never follow through with action. No action toward achieving your decision means no results.

Those same people are inclined to living a mediocre life. A life filled with making positive-decisions will yield positive results.

The bible says faith comes by hearing. You need a positive message to move forward and not give up. That is why the bible says to be ye transformed by the renewing of your mind. Renew your mind using positive thinking, as discussed in *The Secret,* with The Law of Attraction as your guidepost. Remember, always take action steps toward achievement.

Sometimes you have to believe someone else's belief in you until you can believe in yourself. Become the engine that could! Repeat the following affirmations (I think I can, I know I can), with you being the little engine that could, when facing adversity.

In the story about the little engine that could, she (the little engine) had never been over the mountain but knew that she could accomplish the task. The little blue engine that could decided to make it over the mountain, bar none!

By repeating the following positive affirmations, the engine succeeds in pulling the train over the mountain while repeating, 'I think I can, I think I can, I know I can,' make it up the mountain.

We must learn to become the big engine that could, can, and did make it up mountain. Stop! Grab a pen and paper. Make a written list of a minimum of ten positive affirmations that you can repeat to yourself every time you have a mountain to climb. Make it a habit of repeating your affirmations throughout your day, especially every morning, noon, and at night.

The bible says, eyes have not seen, nor ears heard, nor has it entered into the heart of man what God has in store for you. Life will keep going in a direction until you decide to go in another direction.

Every decision that you make counts! God does not treat us like we are robots on an assembly line in a factory. We are independent individuals with the freedom to think as we please, and yes, to make our own decisions.

Have you heard the term – readers are leaders? Leaders make better-informed decisions because of their ongoing personal development. Here are several books designed to help you make better decisions.

I decided to read several leadership books, and I want to share a few of them with you. Let us begin with the original version of *Think and Grow Rich* by Napoleon Hill. *Think and Grow Rich for Women,* by Sharon Lechter. *Think and Grow Rich a Black Choice* by Dr. Dennis Kimbro and Napoleon Hill (after his death). And *How Rich Asians Think* by John Shin.

I am almost sure that you have heard about or read at least one of the books mentioned above. Besides readers being leaders, I am mentioning the *Think and Grow Rich* publications because of the well over 500 documented people that Napoleon Hill interviewed that became the foundation for his content.

Those interviews allowed Hill to develop the content claimed by many successful people (many of them millionaires) as the one book (outside of the bible) that changed their lives.

Decide to read one, if not all, the books mentioned above by the Napoleon Hill Foundation. Only after you complete reading this masterpiece of the master that you are reading right here, right now! I have many more lumps of coal that I will turn in diamonds, filled content, as you read on!!!

Learn as much as you can, and Think And Grow Rich in all areas of your life. You can improve your Health, Spirituality, Wealth, Personal Development, Business Development, Relationships with others, and much more by embracing ongoing self-improvement as a must-have. Remember, we become what we think about, either good, bad, right, or wrong.

Romans 12:2 – "And be ye not conformed to the world but be ye transformed with the renewing of your mind." When we control our thoughts, we can control our destiny. From childhood, we are faced with a multitude of decisions. The process continues from our adolescent experiences to our teenage experience.

We begin to formulate more serious thoughts as young adults, and upon maturity, our decisions seem to come from a wiser place of life experiences. Sometimes through our teen years and young adult years, we make decisions that do not serve us well because we lack knowledge.

Transformational learning can be a critical time for families. Usually, as we mature, our decision-making process gets strategically better. Targeting our focus means making decisions that give our life more clarity, direction, and meaning.

Do not merely coast on autopilot, or you will remain at the same speed. Never going faster, never slowing, never changing lanes, just chugging along.

Your life has meaning! From the day you were born to the day you die. That dash on your tombstone represents your living days from birth to your last breath at death. The dates on your tombstone mean, from the beginning to the end.

While reading your eulogy in front of your family, friends, coworkers, clients, and your church family, the question is, will you be proud of how you lived your life (here on earth) between your dash? How do you want people to remember your life after your death?

Some people decide to go back to school to learn a skill or trade. Others choose to start a new career, or maybe move to another city or country. Some decide to stay in their comfort zone and never change.

They wonder why they cannot do, be, and have their hearts burning desire. Whatever decisions we need to focus on, to make a positive transformation, we must give our thoughts the necessary undivided attention needed throughout each decision-making process.

That focused attention can bring about the desired energy and frequency level needed to make the big difference between the dash in our lives.

Sometimes just making a simple decision to live a peaceful life could be your life's game-changer. There is a scripture that says in Proverbs 21:9 – "It is better to dwell in a corner of a housetop, than to share a house with a contentious woman."

Being in a house with an argumentative, quarrelsome, brawling, combative person is a disaster recipe. Even the constitution of the United States of America says we have a right to Life, Liberty, and the Pursuit of Happiness. Being happy in your home or dwelling is the foundation of every other aspect of your life.

Happiness starts with peace of mind! It is up to you to seek happiness by asking God in prayer. As the older folks used to say, shoot for the stars; if you land on the moon, you are still on higher ground. Some decisions can be significant, while others can be minor.

We often agonize over decisions because they trouble our minds and drain our energy from so much deep seeded thought. What are the pros and cons that are for and against the decisions that must be addressed?

Some decisions may be painful, but often that is where the growth is. Put yourself in a position to take action. When making a decision, your life can change in a split second, when using speed of implementation. Do not become complacent or indecisive! Take immediate action when the opportunity presents itself.

Napoleon Hill did not know that Andrew Carnegie had a stopwatch and was timing Hill's answer to take on the task of interviewing 500 successful men and women for the next twenty years while gathering content for the first Think And Grow Rich Book.

Carnegie gave Hill only 60 seconds to reply. Hill only took 29 seconds before giving Carnegie his (YES) answer. One of Hill's 13 original principals is titled "Procrastination." Remember that procrastination in making decisions is the assassination of obtaining the desired results that you seek!

SHEILATHOUGHTS
THINGS THAT MAKE YOU GO HMMMM

1. What decisions have you made that act as your guidepost or mile marker for your life?

2. How are your past decisions helping you advance in your personal, business, and spiritual life?

3. How quickly do you make decisions?

4. How long do you procrastinate before making decisions?

5. How do you feel when making tough decisions?

6. Are you strong enough to make the right decisions, even though a family member, friend, co-worker, or employee has voiced an opposite point of view?

7. Does your moral compass guide you when you make decisions?

8. When you make the wrong decision that affects others, can you admit your mistake and reverse your decision to make things right?

9. Do you understand that by making no decision, when forced with the opportunity to stand for something, you are deciding to stay on the sidelines and stand for nothing?

10. A decision is a conclusion or resolution reached after consideration of the person, place, or thing that you are faced with, aiding in an eventual outcome.

CHAPTER 6

Swing Until You Hit – Try Again

'Try again' were words that echoed throughout my elementary school years as a young child. I can remember talking so fast that my teachers would say, "can you repeat that, or what did you say?" My neighborhood friends called me motormouth because I would get so wound up and begin talking fast.

'Try again' was also a part of my homework assignment. I would frequently not get my math assignment correct, and I would have to do it again. Try again, and not giving up in many areas of my life became my way of learning. There are many different types of learners. I will share four widely talked about types with you.

- Visual – This type of learner learns by seeing pictures, paintings, diagrams, or other written works. Like the person or note-taker who writes things down all the time.

- Auditory – This type of learner learns best by using sound reinforced teaching or instructions. Their focus is less on reading and writing (even though they do read and write); they would rather listen to the audio sound or the teacher or instructor's voice.

- Kinesthetic – This learning style involves incorporating physical movement into learning activities. This type of learner learns by actively participating and doing things. Activities that people can take part in require them to be on their feet, moving around. Like playing an educational game, for example.
- Reading/writing – This learning style comes from traditional educational concepts, focusing on writing essays, researching, reading, reading, and reading books.

We must discover, understand, and, more importantly, embrace the learning style that best fits our uniqueness.

Nevertheless, we all seem to find our way through the years. The patterns that follow us are the reason why we must keep swinging until we hit. For some, swinging until you hit could mean getting a better paying job, graduating from college, starting a new business or new relationship.

Our memories of trying again sometimes can leave us with lessons learned from the good or a nightmare remembered from the past. There are consequences involved with every decision, sometimes you win, and sometimes you lose!

If you stop swinging until you hit in the game of life, you cannot receive the desired results that you seek.

When you are standing in the batter's box of life, you have positioned yourself to swing at life's opportunities until you hit many of your goals and dreams. Or will you simply stand there and do not swing, while life passes you by, like a 100 mile an hour fastball, that you did not see coming in the form of opportunity?

Do not give up when life seems hard. When the going gets tough, the tough get going! Adopt a belief in yourself that says I am, I can, and I will get all that God wants me to have. I will reach my goals and live my dreams.

Sometimes other people will believe in us more than we believe in ourselves. I'm stating this for a second time because we often dismiss the viewpoint of our abilities and gifts, while others can see and identify our talents. Take on their belief until you can believe in yourself enough to utilize your gifts and talents.

As I stated in an earlier chapter, Jeremiah 29:11 – "For I know the thoughts that I think towards you sayeth the Lord, thoughts of peace and not of evil, to give you an expected end." Jesus thinks of you, and his thoughts of you are pure.

Isaiah 55: 8-9 – "For my thoughts are not your thoughts and your ways are not my ways, says the Lord. For as the heavens are higher than the earth, so are My ways higher than your ways, and My thoughts higher than your thoughts."

God thinks about each of us differently. After all, He created us. God knows what is best for us. Proverbs 19:21 – "There are many devices in a man's heart, nevertheless, the counsel of the Lord that shall stand." In other words, we may make a lot of plans in life, but the Lord will do what He has decided for your life.

The plans that we make that manifest into reality is because God blessed those plans. He wanted you to shine your light in that direction. And the opposite is true for the projects that are not successful. It is God's way of nudging us in another direction, as long as we keep swinging until we hit!

Worrying about things is like attending a negative meditation session in your mind. Galatians 6:9 – "And let us to not grow weary while doing good, for in due season we shall reap if we do not lose heart." In Philippians 1:6 – "Being confident of this very thing, that he which hath begun a good work in you will perform it until the day of Jesus Christ."

And lastly, Philippians 4:13 – "I can do all things through Christ which strengthens me." Jesus can give you the strength to face anything. He can give you the courage to face the difficult decisions that you must make from time to time.

Making tough decisions strengthens your resolve. Expect difficulties when making tough decisions. If everything in life were always smooth sailing all the time, we would have little to no reason for conflict resolutions. There would not be any tough decisions to make.

People who have passion also have higher levels of energy. Using power from your passion helps you to love what you do and do what you love!

You are not defeated when you suffer temporary loss. You are only defeated when you quit. A quitter never wins, and winners never quit! It is about persevering over everything and understanding that you can overcome adversity, trials, and tribulations if you keep swinging until you hit. It will take practice, practice, and more practice, but you can do it.

Most great people in the bible did not get started doing their best work until they were older and wiser. Moses made his best contributions in his early eighties and beyond. Noah was 500 years old when God instructed him to build the ark.

We do not live that long today times. However, Benjamin Franklin invented bifocals at age 76, Harlan "Colonel" Sanders franchised his Kentucky Fried Chicken at age 62, Charles Ranlett Flint launched IBM at age 61. I wanted to name a few of the many older and wiser, late bloomers who kept swinging until they hit. Their companies and brands are still around today as proof positive that age is not a factor.

Do not get discouraged because of your age. History has told the story of many people who got started late, but they kept swinging until they hit or obtained that special something they desired to achieve.

Many people stop when they are three feet from gold, as Sharon Lechter and Greg S. Reid talk about in their book *Three Feet From Gold.* Unbeknownst to a vast number of entrepreneurs, they give up on their dreams while being three feet from accomplishment.

Throughout Discovering Your Uniqueness, I am using a lot of bible verses because I want to remind you of your greatness. The bible is our blueprint for life. By following the Word, its teachings are our clear guide for God's will for our lives.

Focus on the results you want, begin/plan with the end in mind, and stay aligned with your goals and dreams. Keep going and swinging until you hit your opportunity while discovering your greatness.

Do not allow stereotypes, limiting beliefs, and false truths to hold you back from living your best life. Keep swinging until you hit or attract the level of happy relationships, financial empowerment, and positive, like-minded people with the right mindset for success.

Believe that what you think about, you bring about. You are worth more than you realize.

Let us use diamonds as a comparative example. Diamonds come from mines that are dug deep below ground. When diamonds are in their natural state, they usually resemble lumps of pale-colored glass. They often have an oily appearance and do not sparkle. To the untrained eye, they may seem worthless. Once a diamond is cleaned, cut, and polished, it suddenly looks like the apple of her eyes because it now looks more valuable.

On our road to success, we all are diamonds in the

rough. The more we listen, learn, and apply, the help, training, and assistance of those who have blazed the trail of success before us, we eventually begin to clean the cobwebs out of our minds. We cut out bad, non- productive habits while polishing up out acts, on the road to becoming diamonds.

You came from God! You are one of a kind, a unique, unlike no other, wonderfully made person. You are from the dust of the earth through the creation of Adam and Eve. You are more valuable than gold, silver, and diamonds to God. The amount of value you place on yourself is the measure of your power to transform yourself. Just like the transformation of a diamond in the rough to the clear, cut, and polished version of itself, you can do the same.

How do you eat an elephant? One bite at a time. Do not let your failures stop you from seeing your straightforward, clear-cut, polished potential. Develop a strong constitution for yourself, your gifts, and your abilities.

Proverbs 23:7 – "As a man thinketh in his heart so is he." Your thoughts hold the keys to your good, bad, right, or wrong feelings and actions. When you feel that you are at your wit's end, push forward until you experience your breakthrough moment of clarity.

Thomas Edison – "Our greatest weakness lies in giving up. The most certain way to succeed is always to try just one more time" – "I have not failed. I've just found 10,000 ways that won't work". Because he did not quit after 10,000 attempts, Thomas Edison is a household name today!

Abraham Lincoln did not give up even though he failed many times in his life. He Kept trying many different things, but he eventually became the 16th President of the United States. Abraham Lincoln ran for president after enduring many losses in life. Poverty, failed business, nervous breakdown, just to name a few. He kept swinging.

Walt Disney was in deep financial trouble several times while creating, building, and growing his empire. He had a nervous breakdown after creating Mickey Mouse. The famous mouse concept was rejected over 300 times, until one faithful day, Walt Disney received funding. Because Disney kept swinging until he hit, his theme parks are known worldwide. Disney received two honorary degrees (Harvard & Yale) for creating a new language of art.

Be careful about what you affirm, from yourself-to yourself, by way of your thoughts.

Allow yourself the ongoing opportunity to achieve greatness because you kept swinging until you hit. Life is not a picnic; however, it is a process. Failure is a necessary part of growth, as long as you learn from your mistakes.

As mentioned earlier, Colonel Sanders did not launch Kentucky Fried Chicken until the age of 62. Over 1,000 people rejected his chicken recipe. Instead of giving up, the Colonel kept swinging until he hit.

Oprah Winfrey was fired from a job abruptly after a

producer told her she was not fit for television. Oprah went on to become a celebrated talk show host. She launched Harpo Studio in Chicago, and she launched OWN – the Oprah Winfrey Network. Oprah became an actress, executive producer, and published author. Instead of giving up, Oprah kept swinging, and as you can see by her results, she kept on hitting!

It seems like swinging until you hit is a prerequisite for success. It gives you the inner strength and intestinal fortitude needed to achieve the breakthroughs and opportunities required for success in the marketplace.

Sometimes people quit swinging because they do not listen or fail to adopt or grow when the market shifts. Some entrepreneurs display a lack of discipline and lack the necessary persistence to keep swinging until they hit.

It appears that success follows failure if you do not quit. I'm sure you've heard the term "Fail your way to success?" Thomas Edison proved that statement to hold truth and be self-evident.

Even the Beatles of the 1960s experienced rejection by a record company who did not like their sound. Today because John, Paul, George, and Ringo did not quit, an internet source states, the Beatles have sold around 1.6 BILLION singles in the United States and 177 MILLION albums, with worldwide sales topping 600 MILLION.

What if the Beatles would have quit? The same is true

for Michael Jackson and Prince. What if they would have quit? I think I have made my point!

You do not have to be an Abraham Lincoln, Walt Disney, Colonel Sanders, Oprah, The Beatles, Michael Jackson, or Prince. However, you do need to find your passion, make it happen, and do not quit. Remember, Swing Until You Hit – Try Again!

Watching a child learn to walk is an excellent example of trying again. They stumble and fall numerous times before getting it right. Take the time you need to slip, fall, get back up, and heal from failure. You will have bad days from time to time, but do not turn those days into the rest of your life. Get up, brush yourself off, and keep swinging until you hit.

Get the support you need to put yourself back in the batter's box in life! Do not beat yourself up when you encounter failures. Negative self-talk keeps you from growing and causes you to become stagnant. Every experience in life has made you who you are today.

The above examples of 'Swing Until You Hit – Keep Trying' were showcased to energize your quest for success as you seek to achieve that 'special something' that you desire most in life.

Let each example be your source of renewed belief and inspiration. On your road to achievement and success, do not allow someone else's failures, drag you down. Remember, you cannot control how others think, feel, and act, but you can control yourself.

Whatever it is that you want to accomplish, regardless of the struggles, you must become the captain of your ship. You must set your sails in the direction of the powerful winds of success by following principal centered guidepost and roadmaps.

It is true that if you think you can, you can. Success is a failure, turned inside out. You only fail when you quit trying or stop swinging. You cannot hit unless you swing – the word swing means 'take action.'

Put your trust in God. If He told you to do something, believe it is possible. Proverbs 24:16 – "The righteous may fall seven times, but gets up, but the wicked will stumble into trouble." If one door closes, another one will open.

Revelations 3:8 – "I have placed before you an open door that no man can shut it." God is with us to help us. He wants us to succeed. Proverbs 3:5-6 – "Trust in the Lord with all your heart and lean not to your own understanding, in all your ways acknowledge him and he shall direct they paths."

Forget about the past. Stop looking in the rear-view mirror of your life. Think about why the front windshield of your future is larger than the smaller rear-view mirror and rear windshield of your past? It's because what happened in your past is not nearly as important as what can happen in your future.

Press onward towards the results that you seek. It is your birthright to achieve success.

Read the following verse to yourself before you go to bed at night and once again upon waking up. "I can do all things through Christ who strengthens me." – Philippians 4:13. Then, step back into the batter's box of life, and swing until you hit – keep trying!

SHEILATHOUGHTS

THINGS THAT MAKES YOU GO HMMMM

1. Reread the short narratives about Lincoln, Disney, The Beatles, Winfrey, and Sanders, to help you add inspiration and ongoing motivation. Find your inspiration, as well.

2. How often do you look back in the rear-view mirror of your life?

3. When you do look back, do you find the transformational answers that can change your future? If no, what do you see when you look back in your past? Do not dwell on the negative past.

4. What have you been trying to do over and over again?

5. What action steps are you taking to help you reach your goals?

6. Do you have a mentor, coach, or accountability partner that can be your beacon of light along your journey?

7. Do you find yourself giving up too soon?

8. If you answered yes to #7, do you know your WHY?

9. Write down a list of 100 things that you want to accomplish before you pass on from this life. Leave no stone unturned!

10. Look at your list and add dates of accomplishment

that you desire to manifest the things on your list. Out of those 100 things that you listed, you most-likely wrote down your passion. When you find your WHY or desire, only then can you make it happen.

CHAPTER 7

Uniqueness

In a world filled with unlimited opportunities for diversity and inclusion within our global multicultural society, many people feel excluded because of their education, race, color, gender, age, economic status, and religious beliefs. Being excluded from sharing their uniqueness, their cultural experiences, gifts, and talents with the world are insidious.

Psalm 139:17 – "How precious also are the thoughts unto me, oh God, how great is the sum of them." God's thoughts towards His creation is precious. We are the apple of His eye. Our Father and Creator want us to live a value-based, inclusive life to benefit all humanity.

For our global citizens to collectively live a value-based life, the uniqueness of our diversity must be respected and not discriminated. Let us explore what the bible says about value-based inclusion and exclusion between the rich and poor.

James 2:2 – 4 – "For if there comes unto you your assembly a man with a gold ring, in goodly apparel, and there come in also a poor man in vile raiment" – "And ye have respect to him that weareth the gay clothing, and say unto him, Sit thou here in a good place; and say to the poor, Stand thou there, or sit under my footstool" – "Are ye not then partial in yourselves, and becoming judges of evil thoughts?"

While sitting on the tarmac before takeoff, I am sure we all have heard flight attendants explain the safety features for our benefit. One especially important, value-based inclusion is for each passenger to secure his/her oxygen mask first before helping the other person sitting next to you in case of an emergency.

We must first rid ourselves of our bigotry before accepting and inviting others' uniqueness and inclusion into our own lives. W must save or change ourselves first before throwing stones at other people and cultures!

Self-help and personal development are like putting on your oxygen mask. When you learn how to walk, to talk, to breathe, and live by actively doing the things that will make you a better person, from the inside out, your uniqueness and leadership qualities will begin to shine over time.

We were not born to act like sheep. Sheep are always following the leader, even to the slaughterhouse of death. They do not show any resistance; they fall in line and follow along.

Now the Lion is a different breed. The lion earned the title 'King of the jungle.' WHY? Because lions are fearless throughout their journey. They are not the largest animal, nor are they the smartest. However, they are feared the most and are the most daring of all the animals in the jungle.

Are you currently acting like sheep, just following along in life, having little to not goals and dreams? Or are you acting like the lion, fearlessly going for your goals and objectives every day of your journey? Lions never take a day off. Yes, lions rest for hours at a time, but once they are back in the hunt, they play full out, letting nothing stop them?

Og Mandino – "I will persist until I succeed – I was not delivered unto this world into defeat, nor dose failure course my veins. I am not a sheep waiting to be prodded by my shepherd. I am a LION, and I refuse to talk, to walk, to sleep with the sheep. The slaughterhouse of failure is not my destiny – I will persist until I succeed."

It's time to shed the sheepskin wool off your back and replace it with the sight of the lion's distinctive mane. The lion's mane's size serves as a signal to other lions about how strong he might be. The size of your lion's mane can be identified by the level of self-help and personal development fitness that you outwardly express to others.

Do not let your obligation of service to others erode. Your gift is like a jewel inside of you that can shine when you allow it to. Do not limit yourself by not allowing your gift to illuminate and shine bright for yourself, as well as others.

Zig Ziglar –"You can have everything in life that you want if you will just help other people get what they want." Use your gifts to help other people, and the gates of joy and opportunity will rain down upon you.

Think about life as an ocean. There is plenty to explore. Do not limit yourself by wading in the shallow waters with the minnows. Do not be afraid to venture out and swim in the deep sea with Sharks, Whales, Dolphins, and Urchins. Your gifts are a bridge over troubled waters. Your gifts can help you to achieve your destiny. Your gifts can help others achieve their destiny as well.

Learn from the many experiences, disappointments, bumps in the road, setbacks, and failures that you have encountered. During and after your learning curve, you can help change the world and have a more significant impact on our global citizens. Do not allow the thought of unworthiness or insecurities to hold you back from your uniqueness. Remember; be like the lion, FEARLESS!

Sometimes the fear of failure or another disease called excusitis can hold a person back from displaying their authentic self. This limited belief and negative thinking can lead to a pattern of paralysis of positive thoughts.

Sometimes God allows a situation to come along to bring out our skill or ability. We do not always know what is in us until we are tested or challenged. I love seeing people pulling together to help other people when confronted with difficult situations and challenges.

During catastrophic tragedies, people from all walks of life come together for the greater good. Sadly to say – it takes a tragedy to bring out diversity and inclusion to the forefront of survival on a grand scale.

Like the unforgettable experience in New York City in 2001, on September 11th. Two planes were flown into the World Trade Center's twin towers, while a third plane hit the Pentagon outside of Washington, D. C. A fourth plane crashed in the open field in Shanksville, Pennsylvania.

In every instance, people united and pulled together to assist each other during this horrific moment in history. The human spirit is strong and resilient. Many heroic and great stories came out of those tragic events.

If you tried to reconstruct your mind mechanically, it would cost you billions of dollars. Example: In 2010, IBM introduced a supercomputer named 'Watson' to the world. Watson has a combination of artificial intelligence (AI) with software to be 'a question-answering machine.' The developmental cost to create Watson is estimated to be between $900 million to $1.8 billion.

Your gift is your source of uniqueness and significance. How you use your gift is what makes you unique. Using our gifts to help or entertain others, gives our life meaning. What makes Lebron James or Stephan Curry great basketball players? It was their gift of having superior athletic talent and skills in the sport of basketball. Athletes get paid well because they know how to monetize their gift.

Your gift comes from God. Your skills will always be inside you until you understand how to use them. Your job may not be the perfect situation that allows your gifts shine. Do not allow anyone to make you feel unworthy of your contributions. Because of your talents, others see you as being a significant contributor to society.

At one point in Michael Jordan's short-lived college career, his coach, Dean Smith, did not know the real value of Jordan's exceptional gift. Because Michael was a freshman, Coach Smith understood the growing pains of playing high school to college basketball.

Michael Jordan (using the tenacity of a lion) kept practicing. He kept putting in the work. When preparedness and opportunity meet, the by-product is success.

During Jordan's freshman year at North Carolina, he hit the game-winning shot in the 1982 NCAA Championship tournament victory over Patrick Ewing's Georgetown team. Would you agree that Michael Jordan's gift made others see him as being unique and significant? Your gift can do the same for you along your journey in life.

The bible says your gift will make room for you and bring before great men. Using your gift to its fullest potential will serve others, as well as add zeros to your bank account. Opportunity is always around for those who seek her favor!

When you find your moment of clarity, you can use your gift inside of you to help better others' lives. When you do not use your gift, guess what it's doing? Your gift is screaming, scratching, clawing, and trying to dig its way out from being trapped inside of you. Your gift wants to be free to help and serve others on a higher level.

Three wise men were discussing the best place to hide the special gift, that if man searched for it, they would not find it until they were ready to receive it! Gifts are special. Gifts from God, delivered to us at birth, should be used for the greater good of everyone.

Let's see how the three of us can solve this riddle using our three gifts from God: knowledge, wisdom, and understanding.

The first wise man said, we can hide the gift at the bottom of the deepest ocean – no way, because man can use a submarine and dive to the depths of the ocean floor and find the gift.

The second wise man said we could hide the gift on the moon – no way because man can blast off in a spaceship, land on the moon, walk on the moon, and find the gift.

The third wise man said, I know where to hide the gifts – we can hide the gift inside of man – where they will be hidden in plain sight! Until each man or woman discovers his or her gift, we need not worry because man will never find it.

You must look and explore deep within our mind, body, and soul to find your unique gift. It all starts with your mirror image's self-reflection that is staring back at you every time you look in the mirror.

Like all the phenomenally successful people mentioned throughout this book as examples, they discovered their unique gifts and talents. Maybe you do not want to achieve their level of success, and that is alright! However, you can achieve that 'special something' that you desire.

The citizens of our global planet can have access to something you created because you stepped up to the plate, and you kept swinging until you hit your special gift out of the park.

Strive to achieve excellence in all that you do. God put Adam in the garden. He did not build a house out of the forest, but the lumber was there, hidden in the trees. The gold, silver diamonds, and precious metals were there, hidden in the soil. These elements are gifts from God.

God gave intellect and man's ability to make good, bad, right, or wrong decisions. The repercussions of our choices have and always will have a positive or negative impact on our environment. Generation after generation, man's intellect continued evolving while growing and expanding, bringing with it new frontiers for humanity's benefit.

With the never-ending improvement of human intelligence, great inventions came with new knowledge and experiments. Today we experience many comforts because of man's continued growth and ability to experiment while working with new ideas from thought.

George Washington Carver was an agricultural scientist and inventor. Carver discovered or invented over 300 uses for the peanut. Because of one of God's many gifts to the world (the peanut) and the fact that George Washington Carver found the gift that was inside of him, humanity still benefits today.

Not only must we talk the talk, but we must also walk the walk. Meaning, we must use our gifts to help serve the needs of others! It's not just about what we say; it's more about what we do with our gifts.

The Bible says that the Lord God took the man (Adam) and put him in the garden of Eden to tend and keep it. That was Adam's job. Whatever God calls you to do, He will provide. What God demands; He supplies. Adam had it within him to do the work. God would not have told him to do something he was not capable of achieving.

Whatever God expects of you, He injects in you. Your gift can help create your dream of service to others, your dream salary, and your dream lifestyle. Your gift makes you special because you are unique and wonderfully made.

Once you decide to be, do, and have 'that special something' that your heart desires, the way will present itself. Even people incarcerated behind prison walls still have their gifts. Some of their gifts are the reasons why they were arrested by law enforcement.

Some have gifts of singing, writing, drawing, or teaching. Even though they made some costly mistakes, some of the most remarkable contributions have come from X-offenders who turned their life around after being given a second chance.

Like Kweisi Mfume, he went to jail several times before becoming a United States Congressman and serving as president of the NAACP. A former hacker named Mitnick was once on the FBI's Most Wanted List before launching his security firm. Judge Greg Mathis served time behind bars before being appointed to the bench.

You might know an X-offender who turned his or her life around and are doing great things after finding their moment of clarity and discovering their uniqueness.

God is not dependent on us; we are dependent on Him. People may not know or like you, but they will pay you for your gift. People may not like going to the dentist, but the dentist earns good money for their skills. So, whatever you do, search for your gifts until you find them.

The 1964 Nobel Peace Prize recipient, Dr. Martin Luther King Jr. — "If you can't fly, run. If you can't run, walk. If you can't walk, crawl, but whatever you do, you have to keep moving forward."

Refine your gift so that you can become valuable to our global community. Dr. Martin Luther King also said, (paraphrased) — You want to do your job so well that the angels lean over and say that you are the best at what you do.

Always remember, you were born unique, fearfully, and wonderfully made. You are far more than just a human being. You are a masterpiece because you are a piece of the master. You were born to think, create, invent, and yes, serve people's needs. And when that happens, you will be paid handsomely for your efforts. Do not abandon your uniqueness and the gift that God has given you!

SHEILATHOUGHTS

THINGS THAT MAKES YOU GO HMMMM

1. Think about and imagine how the power of your gifts can help serve the needs of others. Do not procrastinate.

2. Identify your gift and talents.

3. Decide on which gift is your passion and decide to make it happen.

4. What are some things you can do to enhance your gift?

5. Take total responsibility for your success and your failures.

6. Complete your due diligence while developing your gift.

7. Form a think tank or mastermind group to help guide you.

8. Develop your mission statement concerning your gift.

9. Develop an action plan that you will follow when using your gifts and talents.

10. Who can help coach or mentor you to help you develop your gift?

EPILOGUE

Now that you read this book, you have more than enough real-life and spiritual examples to guide you along your journey. I added the fictional story about Rudolph the Red-nosed Reindeer and the Little Engine That Could, so can share with your children in the form of Discovering Your Uniqueness on their level of thinking and understanding.

Each story throughout this book speaks to your thoughts, feelings, and emotional intelligence. The journey of one thousand miles begins with the first step, meaning you must take action!

My call to action challenge for you is this:

When you look in the mirror of your life, do you see Uniqueness in you? If Yes, make it your daily mission to use self-help and personal development to keep you sharp! Use the wisdom, knowledge, and understanding of your trusted think-tank or mastermind group to help hold you accountable.

If you answered no: Start right where you are today. Start with the man/woman in the mirror and make that transformational decision to change. You cannot continue to do the same things and expect different results.

More importantly - seek out a mentor or coach, a think-tank, or mastermind group of like-minded accountability partners who blazed the trail before you. If you do not know something, begin asking questions. The only bad question is the question that you do not ask. Think about and imagine what your legacy will be? What you will be remembered for at the end of your dash, between life and death, depends on what you do today!

ABOUT THE AUTHOR

S heila White is an award-winning film and television producer for Road 2 Eternity, located in the United States. She is a former radio host for Christian Lifestyle Radio Network.

Sheila is a member of a local community access television station funded by Comcast and the president of a non-for-profit organization called 'Go On And Live,' which provides valuable resources to businesses, individuals, and ministries.

She is the Vice President of Lightcore Animation, a company that produces innovative, uplifting, and entertaining stories through animated media. Sheila is an administrator for Skyward Books and is a member of JD3TV, a streaming television service. Sheila is married with three children and lives in the Chicagoland area in the United States.

Printed in the United States
By Bookmasters